Rainforest Math

Written by Claire Owen

Costa Rica

My name is Rosa. I live in Costa Rica. Can you think of any animals that live in the rainforest? What is your favorite animal? Where does it live?

Contents

Wherever you see me, you'll find activities to try and questions to answer.

Rainforest Riches

Costa Rica is a small country—a little smaller than the state of West Virginia. However, Costa Rica has rainforests rich in plant and animal life. In fact, there are more species of plants and animals in Costa Rica than in the whole of Europe! Costa Rica has set aside about one-fourth of its total area for parks and reserves. This is a greater fraction than any other country in the world.

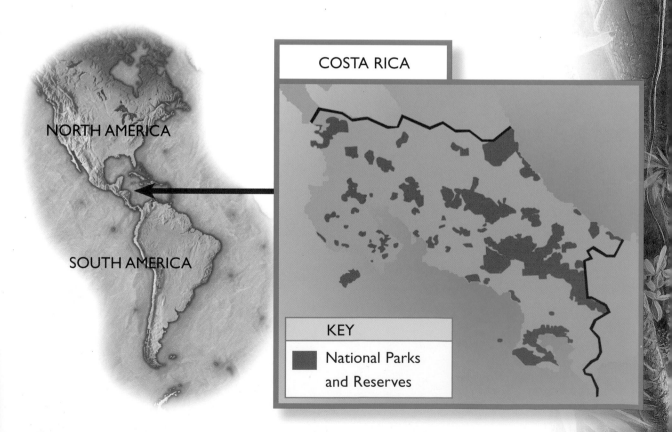

COSTA RICA

NORTH AMERICA

SOUTH AMERICA

KEY

National Parks and Reserves

species a group of plants or animals of the same kind

Number of Animal Species in Costa Rica

Class of Animal	More Than:
Amphibians	150
Birds	850
Insects	35,000
Mammals	200
Reptiles	200

What do you notice about the order of the information in the chart above? Make a new chart that shows the numbers in order, from least to greatest.

Record Holders

Some of the world's most interesting creatures live in the Costa Rican rainforest. The howler monkey is the world's noisiest animal. The three-toed sloth is the slowest mammal in the world. The goliath bird-eating spider is the world's biggest spider. The rhinoceros beetle is the world's strongest creature for its size.

The howler monkey's call can be heard clearly from 3 miles away.

On the ground, the three-toed sloth often takes about one minute to travel 4 yards.

The rhinoceros beetle can carry 850 times its own weight!

The goliath bird-eating spider weighs more than 6 ounces and has a legspan of 10 inches.

Figure It Out

How would you solve these wacky problems? You may use a calculator to help.

1. Mighty Max is as strong as a rhinoceros beetle! He weighs 60 pounds. Could Max carry a 50,000-pound bus?

2. How many goliath bird-eating spiders would fit side by side across your classroom?

3. Harry the howler monkey is visiting a friend who lives 5,000 yards away. Will Harry be able to hear his mother call him for dinner? (Hint: 1 mile = 1,760 yards)

4. How many minutes would it take for a three-toed sloth to travel from your classroom to the lunchroom? (You could use a yardstick to measure the distance.)

Beautiful Butterflies

Costa Rica is home to about one-tenth of the world's butterfly species. Perhaps the most famous of these is the blue morpho. Surprisingly, the tiny scales that cover the blue morpho's wings are not blue! The color comes from light reflecting off ridges on the scales.

The blue morpho's wings are brown underneath, with "eyes" that scare away enemies.

reflect   to send back light rays from a surface

Use a ruler to measure each butterfly's wingspan to the nearest half-inch. (These pictures are life-size.) Make a chart to show the measurements.

Small postman

Queen cracker

Owl butterfly

wingspan   the distance between the wingtips of a bird, insect, or airplane

Wide Wingspans

The largest butterfly in the Costa Rican rainforest is the owl butterfly. However, the largest butterfly in the world is the Queen Alexandra's birdwing. This poisonous butterfly from Papua New Guinea has a wingspan of 11 inches!

The male (top) and female (bottom) Queen Alexandra's birdwing

With a wingspan of half an inch, the pygmy blue is the world's smallest butterfly. How many pygmy blue butterflies would fit across one birdwing butterfly?

Enlarge a Butterfly

To make a life-sized paper birdwing, you will need a piece of one-inch grid paper. (Ask your teacher for a copy from the Teacher's Notes.)

Follow these steps to enlarge the picture below.

1. Take a sheet of one-inch grid paper.
2. Copy one square at a time from the half-inch grid below to your one-inch grid. Use a pencil so you can erase mistakes!
3. Color your butterfly and cut it out.

Amazing Ants

Ants are the most abundant creatures in the rainforest. One of the most interesting ants in Costa Rica is the leaf-cutter ant. These ants use their jaws to cut leaves into small pieces. They carry the pieces back to their nest and chew them up to make compost. The ants use the compost to grow a white fungus that they eat.

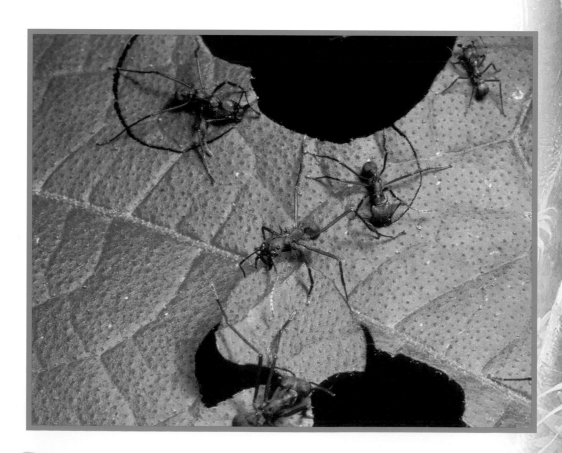

abundant   present in great quantities or numbers

Leaf-cutter ants build huge underground nests. Up to 5 million ants live in a single nest! The largest nests can be 20 feet deep and 30 feet across. From their nest, the ants make paths up to 300 feet long. Each day, they clear away leaves and twigs from these ant highways.

Army ants travel in huge groups. It can take several hours for the thousands of ants in an "army" to pass by!

Amazing Anteaters

With so many ants, it's not surprising that Costa Rica is home to several species of anteater. These long-nosed animals use their sharp claws to rip open the nests of ants and termites. Then they use their long, skinny tongues to lick up thousands of ants.

The lesser anteater, or tamandua, has a beautiful gold and black coat.

The giant anteater has stiff, strawlike hair that grows up to 16 inches long on its tail.

Figure It Out

Read Juan's report about the giant anteater. Match each of the letters (A through G) with a logical entry from the Missing Data list.

Missing Data

4 feet

24 inches

30,000

65 pounds

4 inches

150

3 feet

The Giant Anteater   by Juan

The giant anteater weighs about _____ A _____ .
The length of its body is about _____ B _____ ,
and its bushy tail adds another _____ C _____ !
The anteater has very strong forearms with
sharp claws about _____ D _____ long. Its tongue
can reach about _____ E _____ into an ant nest.
The giant anteater can flick its tongue in
and out about _____ F _____ times per minute!
Each day, it eats about _____ G _____ ants.

Sample Answers

Page 5   The order is alphabetical.

150; 200; 200; 850; 35,000

Page 7   1. Yes

3. Yes

Page 9   Small postman: 2 inches

Queen cracker: 3.5 inches

Owl butterfly: 6 inches

Page 10   22

Page 15

A: 65 pounds	B: 4 feet
C: 3 feet	D: 4 inches
E: 24 inches	F: 150
G: 30,000	

Do some research about another animal from Costa Rica. Write a report with blanks (like Juan's on page 15). Make a list of missing data.

Index